TOUCHSTONES

Volume 1

Texts for Discussion

Selected, translated, and edited

by

Geoffrey Comber
Nicholas Maistrellis
Howard Zeiderman

CZM Press

CZM Press
Suite 104, 48 West Street
Annapolis, MD 21401

©1985, 1986, 1995

Printed in Canada

Third Edition, 1995

ISBN 1-878461-34-6

Cover Design by Adrienne Rogers

Table of Contents

INTRODUCTION

All of us, teachers and students alike, recognize those moments when a class suddenly comes to life. On those occasions, all our normal classroom roles dissolve. For five or ten minutes, students who never speak get actively involved, the teacher learns as well as teaches, and normally active students cooperate with their less active classmates. These moments are exciting, and real learning takes place. But they are usually accompanied by confusion and a sense of being left up in the air. These discussions may not reach definite conclusions or any clear agreement. It may even be that no one is sure how to ask the right questions. The teacher may feel irresponsible because normal classwork is not being covered. The pressure of next week's test is always present. The students may feel puzzled because they are not being taught and guided in the way they expect. Things seem to be on the verge of getting out of hand, so everyone feels somewhat relieved when the usual situation of active teachers teaching passive students is restored.

Yet, those rare exciting times when everyone in the room is involved in learning are what we remember as the most important moments in school. We all wish that what seemed to happen by chance could happen regularly and more often. The project outlined here attempts to bring this about, but without the confusion that we feel when having such spontaneous discussions. The goal of this project is not just

to have more of these exciting moments in school. The goal
is that all aspects of learning take on a new purpose and
importance, changing our whole attitude toward school. The
Touchstones project enables this to happen by encouraging
regular discussions of a very special kind.

I. GOALS

The Touchstones Discussion Project reorients students
and teachers toward education. From their earliest years in
school, students must begin to learn how to teach themselves.
It is no longer sufficient that our pupils become good students
who master particular facts and skills. Skills of a higher order
are necessary to flourish in an increasingly technological
world. As teachers, we should confront this necessity as an
opportunity.

It has always been our aim that our students share with
us the responsibility for their education. Yet we have
frequently had to subordinate this aim to the specific curricular
goals which fill the school day. No sustained effort has been
made to direct the emerging curiosity, initiative, and
independence of our students so that they become more active
collaborators in their own educations. However, the emerging
professional, economic and technological world requires that
we teachers turn our implicit aim to a reality. This aim is no
longer a luxury for a few students but a requirement for all of
them. The Touchstones Discussion Project creates a carefully
designed environment within which the skills necessary for
students to collaborate with us and teach themselves are
introduced, practiced, and mastered. It is an environment
within which all students, regardless of their apparent ability
level, can achieve skills which previously few if any students
mastered.

The weekly Touchstones class makes collaboration

possible by creating an academic environment in which the participants experience how our interdependence is necessary for the success of the activity. In a Touchstones class, students are not viewed individually as talented or untalented, skilled or unskilled. *All* students have both strengths and weaknesses. All contribute their respective strengths and assist one another to compensate for and correct their respective weaknesses. In addition, the opinions, experiences, desires, fears, and uncertainties of our students animate and bring out the substance in the texts considered. They begin to desire to collaborate with us generally in school because in this specific instance they find they have had the adequate knowledge and skill to take the initiative in an academic context.

Though participation in weekly Touchstones discussions can instill in students the desire to collaborate with us and each other, a mere desire does not achieve serious and sustained initiatives. This step requires incorporating a new set of expectations about their responsibilities and ours, and a new set of skills with which they can achieve these new goals. Through the Touchstones discussion format, our long-range goal for students—that they someday cease being merely students and become able to teach themselves—can be incorporated into their educational experience. Though discussions will not and should not be the principal method of teaching subject areas, Touchstones discussion classes can create a framework of expectations whose goal is that students learn how to learn: that is, that they learn how to teach themselves.

Learning how to learn is a complex process that requires the development of many skills. Touchstones classes develop these skills through the systematic use of individual and small-group work and through full-class discussion.

Though students will learn how to participate in discussions, this important ability is not an end in itself. Rather, in the weekly Touchstones class, students exercise skills that increase their ability to gain from their regular classes. For example, they learn to

* work with others regardless of background,
* understand what it means to support opinions with evidence,
* take responsibility for their opinions,
* be comfortable when confronted with new situations,
* respect other people's opinions,
* respect themselves, and
* listen to, analyze, and think about problems that do not have complete and simple solutions.

These are the kinds of skills we most commonly need in our own lives.

II. THE SCOPE OF THE TOUCHSTONES PROJECT

Touchpebbles for elementary schools introduces the skills of active learning through exercises that emphasize the imaginative manipulating, completing, or rewriting of texts. Middle school and particularly high school students are capable of dealing actively with texts by analysis and reflection. Younger students, however, need more tangible devices for doing the same things. Such devices take many forms in Touchpebbles. In *Touchpebbles: Volume B*, students are asked to complete a text, or to reconstruct a story from parts, or to complete and orient an abstract painting. The lessons in *Touchpebbles: Volume A* offer two or more perspectives on the same topic, subject, or issue. In both volumes, a written text or work of art is actively and cooperatively worked on by students both individually and in groups. Through this work, students begin to explore teaching themselves and each other. They find they have more to contribute than they expected, they learn to work actively with texts, they experience the continual interplay of reasoning and imagining in intellectual exploration, and they realize that the school environment is an integral part of their daily interests and concerns.

Touchstones for middle schools introduces group discussion, active listening, and active reading more systematically. The exercises and class work activities in Touchstones for middle schools are directive and structured. The middle school approach allows discussion to be practiced in a variety of different contexts without requiring students to focus on them directly . Thus, the texts in Touchstones for middle schools are not specifically the focus of attention. The texts draw attention to the students' experiences and opinions. In this format, the students learn to discuss and to explore what they have taken for granted. They become motivated learners.

Finally, in **Touchstones for high schools**, these cooperative skills are practiced through activities designed to make students explicitly aware of the presuppositions of their own thoughts, of their responses toward the remarks of others, and of their attitudes towards the opinions expressed in the texts. Their tendency is to be either contemptuous of the opinions of other people or too accepting of the printed word. These tendencies are checked by exercises that encourage and guide students to view a given opinion as one of many possible views they can entertain in a specific situation. Once the possibility of multiple opinions becomes real for students, they can master the skills of cooperating and listening.

III. CHARACTERISTICS OF THE TOUCHSTONES CLASS

1. *Role of the Leader*

A discussion on a Touchstones text reveals tension between the text and students. It also reveals that tension exists among the students. The leader's role is to keep the tension from moving students too far away from the text on the one hand or from their experiences on the other. If the leader uses the text as a means to jump to some abstract issue (such as, Is the will free? or, Is the individual more important than the society?), the discussion will lose focus. The leader will have to bring the discussion back to the text. If the discussion stays too long on a small detail in the text, the leader should ask why this detail is important and ask for an example from students' lives. On the other hand, if students are simply trading stories or experiences with one another, the leader must ask them to relate the story or experience to the text.

The leader does not direct the discussion; the leader creates and preserves the conditions for a discussion, that is, makes sure everyone is responsible to the text and to one another. It is best when everyone does this for each other and themselves. When that happens, each takes on the role of leader.

The leader does not summarize the discussion. Everyone is free to have an opinion about what was said in the discussion. Almost always the conversation will go on in the corridors or at home.

Finally, neither the teacher nor students should be afraid of long silences. Let them happen. They are the times when more thought goes on that will make the discussion which follows better.

2. *Opening Question*

The discussion begins with a question asked by the teacher, though sometimes a student may do this. The Touchstones texts are complex and rich, and the opening question can begin anywhere in the text. As the class follows the issue opened up by the question, gradually many other issues in the text will be touched on. As there is not just one theme or one issue in any text, so there is not one and only one opening question. Many possible questions will be able to lead us over the fabric of the text.

A good opening question is brief and honest. It must be a real concern of the person asking it. But once begun, the discussion takes on a life of its own, and the opening question may soon be absorbed by the other questions which will be raised.

3. *Outside Information*

If all outside information is forbidden from discussions, only a dry and formal exchange would take place. Value would then reside exclusively in the ability of students to unravel and master the details of a text. The students who can do this well will certainly be the same ones who are skilled in their regular classes, that is, the ones who usually give good answers to the teacher's questions. This might give an illusion of a discussion, but the members of the class will be playing the same roles as usual. They will speak to one another through the teacher. There will be no cooperative learning. No real change will have occurred.

However, if all kinds of outside information are allowed, another sort of difficulty shows up. For example, if we go on and on talking only about personal experiences, the result will be a rap session, not a real discussion. This is not a way to reflect on our most strongly held beliefs and assumptions. If many historical facts are brought into the discussion, then everyone must listen to the historical "expert," and again discussion stops. If newspaper accounts of recent politics are introduced, then the discussion will almost surely become a hotly contested debate. But a debate is not at all similar to a discussion.

Therefore, some kind of outside information and personal experience must be brought in. The only questions are, what kind and how? First and foremost, it must be something everyone can share in. Even a personal experience should be understandable to everyone so that everyone sees how it bears on the question. Both the speaker and the listener must take responsibility for the relevance of each remark. The speaker must be responsible for what is said, and the listener must be responsible for treating it with respect. We are not playing games or acting out roles. All must try to say what they really mean, and strive hard to understand what others say. Therefore, it is important that whatever outside information is offered, be it a story, an experience, or a historical fact, it must be connected to the text. It must shed light on the text, as an illustration or a contrast. Whatever is said must be public and available to everyone, and lead to a greater understanding of the text and our relation to it. It should never be the kind of remark which brings discussion to a stop.

4. *Context for Discussion*

The purposes of Touchstones discussions are to train us to converse reflectively, to think critically, to analyze concepts, and finally to share the responsibility for learning with one another. Conversing, thinking, analyzing and being responsible are skills and habits which, like all skills and habits, are best learned through regular practice. Everyone should learn them because everyone needs these skills and habits in life. But for this to happen, discussions will need to be held regularly—perhaps once a week. They should, however, be separate from the normal classes such as mathematics, social studies, or English. There are two reasons for this.

First, since the texts in Touchstones are about issues that concern us all, we should not turn to experts for answers. We all know something about wanting revenge, feeling alone, what a point or a line is, and what it feels like when you finally understand something. We all have something worthwhile to contribute to discussions of these questions, but no one has *the answer*. For this reason the teacher needs to give up the role of authority figure which is proper in normal classes. For the same reason, the usual labels of students are inappropriate. It doesn't matter if students are gifted or non-gifted, advanced or remedial, quick or slow. It does matter if they are courageous or timid, cooperative or selfish, sensitive or insensitive. We must learn to listen to everyone, and accept criticism from everyone. We must learn to use and build on the thoughts of others; act as a bridge between others; think seriously without reaching a definite conclusion; relate particular experiences to general concepts.

Second, the texts in this book do not fit easily into such ordinary categories as English, social studies, or mathematics. They overflow our usual boundaries. Each text can be read from many points of view. However, it would be difficult to do this in a normal class, especially when reading the text for the first time. The tendency would be to read it from one perspective and to ignore all the others. This diminishes and harms the text by restricting possible approaches. Each of these texts has so many perspectives and permits so many approaches, that Touchstones discussions are both possible and even necessary . After a text has been considered in a Touchstones discussion, however, it could be read again in the context of one or more regular classes. At that stage, with more and more practice, groups can focus on reading from a given perspective, and use it to reach more detailed conclusions which can supplement the Touchstones approach.

5. *Organization of the Room*

In a Touchstones discussion, students and teachers move from their usual arrangement into a circle. It is important to see one another. Discussions occur face to face. In addition, the circular arrangement makes it harder to have side conversations. Nothing damages a discussion more than a few people whispering while someone else bravely tries to explore personal beliefs. When these private exchanges occur, everyone becomes unwilling to take risks publicly. A discussion on Touchstones texts makes possible and requires cooperation, courage, and mutual respect. This is what is involved in taking responsibility for oneself and for a class.

TOUCHSTONES
TEXTS

1.   *The Iliad*, Bk. VI,
by Homer

    In the tenth year of the war between the Greeks and Trojans, Agamemnon, leader of the Greeks, insulted Achilles, their greatest warrior. While Achilles, furious, refused to fight, the Trojans led by Hector became bolder than they had ever been. For the first time in ten years, they began fighting the Greeks away from the city. Yet, even as they won small victories, all the Trojans feared that Achilles, who had killed so many of them, would return to fight and catch them out in the open.

    After one of the battles, Hector returned to the city looking for his wife, Andromache. He found her with their infant son above the city gate. They stood together holding hands and looked at their child. Hector smiled in silence but Andromache had tears in her eyes as she began to speak. "Your great courage will be what kills you. And you have no pity for me and your son. When the Greeks destroy you it would be better if I die too. Without you, there is nothing for me but sorrow. In one battle Achilles killed my father and seven brothers. On the day he finally released my mother for ransom, she also died. You, my husband, are now also father, mother, and brother to me. Don't make your child an orphan. Don't let your wife become a widow. Draw your men up to the fig tree near the city. Don't go down and fight in the open spaces near the ships."

    Hector, wearing his shining bronze armor, answered her. "I think about that too, woman, but how could I face my men and their wives if I stayed away from the battle. And my own spirit won't let me. Ever since I learned to fight, I've always been the best of the Trojans. I've won a great name for myself and my father. And there's one thing I know. A day will come when this city will be destroyed and my father's people will perish. And though my brothers and parents will be killed, I think about you most of all. On that day a Greek will lead you away in tears. You will be a slave in someone's home. Someday, seeing you cry, a Greek will say, 'This is the wife of Hector, greatest of the Trojans'. I pray that before I hear you crying as they take you away, I will be dead and buried in the ground."

As Hector finished, he held out his arms for his baby boy. The child screamed and pressed back harder against his nurse's bosom. His father frightened the boy, since his head was covered by a bronze helmet with a horse-hair plume like some strange animal. Hector and Andromache both laughed. The smiling warrior took off his helmet and picked up his son. He tossed him in the air and kissed him. He looked up to the sky and prayed, "Let my boy be as I am, first among the Trojans. Someday let men say of him, 'He is better by far than his father when he comes home from battle.'"

Notes *(while reading)*

Opening question *(after reading)*

Comments *(after discussion)*

2. *About Revenge,*
by F. Bacon

Revenge is a sort of savage justice. The more people try to take revenge, the more the law should punish them. When a man commits a crime, he breaks the law. But when the injured person takes revenge, the person destroys law itself. In taking revenge, a person does indeed get even with his enemy. But when one refuses to take revenge, he shows that he is better than his enemy. King Solomon, I am sure, said it is glorious for a person to forget an injury.

Whatever is past is gone and can't be changed. Wise people know they have enough to do in the present and with whatever might happen in the future. They don't spend their time taking revenge. People who spend their time worrying about past injuries just waste their time. Also, no person hurts another person just to hurt him. Rather, it is done for his profit or his own pleasure or his honor or for some other reason he might have. So why should I be angry with someone for loving himself better than he loves me? Suppose someone hurts me because he is evil. Isn't that just like a thorn or briar which scratches me because it can't do anything else?

Revenge is most allowable when there is no specific law to correct an injury. However, one must then be careful that the kind of revenge one takes does not break another law.

Some people when they get even want their enemy to know that it will happen. This is a more generous way of acting. Not letting your enemy know you are going to get even is a cowardly thing to do. It is like killing at night from ambush.

There was an Italian ruler, Cosimo de Medici, who

said the following to his friends who might betray or injure him: "We read," he said, "that we are commanded to forgive our enemies. But we never read that we are commanded to forgive our friends." I think, however, that the spirit of what Job said is truer. He said, "Shall we receive good from God and not also be willing to accept the evil"? The same is true, in part, about friends.

What is certain about planning to get even is that one's own wounds remain open. If one didn't spend one's time trying to take revenge, those injuries would heal and be forgotten. Public or state revenges are, for the most part, good—as in the case of the murderers of Julius Caesar. Private revenges are, however, not good. People who take revenge live the life of witches. They cause trouble to others and come to a bad end.

Notes *(while reading)*

Opening question *(after reading)*

Comments *(after discussion)*

3.   *Physics*, Bk. II, Ch. 7

by Aristotle

When we see something which interests us, whether it is a natural thing or a man-made thing, we try, above all, to understand it. We don't think we *really* understand something until we understand *why* it is the way it is. Another way of saying this is that when we see something which makes us wonder, we want to know what *causes* it. However, it is pretty clear that the word *cause* means many different things. Let us try to list these different things, and see which are the most important.

First, the material out of which something is made causes the thing to be what it is. For example, the stone out of which a statue is made causes the statue to be what it is. It would be very different if it were made out of wood.

Second, the shape or the pattern of something is also a cause of it being what it is. For example, if someone asks you how you know that a certain figure is a triangle, you will probably say that it looks like a triangle, that it has the shape of a triangle.

Third, anything which is responsible for something else is the cause of it. For example, the father and mother are causes of the baby. The sculptor causes the statue. If you ask someone for advice and when he gives it you follow it, this person causes your action.

Fourth, cause means the goal something or someone is aiming at. This kind of cause I call the *final cause* because it is the most important of all the causes. If you exercise and someone asks you why, you say, "in order to be healthy". If someone asks why geese fly south every autumn, the most important answer is, "in order to get to some place warm for the winter." Finally, if someone asks why a tool, an axe, has a particular shape, the best answer is that it is shaped that way in order to cut wood.

In all these cases the other meanings of cause also apply. For example, if someone asks why geese fly south in the autumn, other answers are that they are made out of strong muscles and light bones, or that they have wings, or that the days have grown very short and cold. All these answers are true, but the most important answer is that it is good for them to be in warm places when winter arrives. This is the final cause. It tells you what something is good for, and this is what you really want to know.

Notes *(while reading)*

Opening question *(after reading)*

Comments *(after discussion)*

4.   *The Histories,*
by Herodotus

Croesus, the king of Lydia, made war on all the cities in Ionia and Aeolia, and conquered them. Over the next few years he brought all the neighboring nations under his control. When all these nations became part of the Lydian empire, the wealth and strength of Sardis, the capital of Lydia, was at its greatest. At that time some wise men from Greece visited king Croesus. One of them was Solon, from the Greek city of Athens. Croesus put Solon up in his royal palace as his guest. After a few days, the Lydian King made a point of showing his visitors the greatness of his wealth and strength. Croesus said to Solon, "You have traveled to many lands, and are said to be wise. Who is the happiest man you have ever seen?" He asked this because he thought he was the happiest and wanted Solon to admit it. However, Solon answered, "Tellus of Athens, sir." Croesus was surprised, and asked why. Solon said, "Because he had good, handsome sons, and he lived to see them all grow up. His life was comfortable. He died courageously in battle to keep his city free, and the Athenians gave him a public funeral, and praised him highly."

Croesus asked a second time, "Solon, who, after Tellus, seems happiest?", expecting he would be given at least a second place. But Solon said, "Cleobis and Bito from Argos. They had all they needed and were both very good athletes. They won many prizes at the Olympic Games. They loved their mother and honored her in public. When they died, their mother and all the other women of Argos praised and honored them."

After two disappointments, Croesus spoke angrily, "Solon! Do you really believe that these common men were happier than I am?" Solon replied, "King Croesus, how can I tell if you are happy until I hear how you have died? If someone is healthy, does not have bad luck, has fine children, is good-looking, and then has a good death, he may really be called happy. But you can't call someone's life happy until it is finished. In everything we must always look at the end. Often a man is given a gleam of happiness and then ruined." These thoughts did not please Croesus. He let Solon leave convinced that the Greek wise man was a fool.

Notes *(while reading)*

Opening question *(after reading)*

Comments *(after discussion)*

5.   *Continuity and Irrational Numbers,*
by R. Dedekind

I say that all of arithmetic is a natural result of the simple act of counting. And counting is nothing other than the creation, one after another, of the series of positive numbers or integers such as 1, 2, 3, 4 and so on. This series does not end. It is infinite. The simplest arithmetic act is creating a new number, say 5, from an already created number, in this case 4.

The chain or series of these numbers is a very useful tool for the human mind. It contains a vast collection of laws and truths once we introduce the four basic operations of arithmetic: addition, subtraction, multiplication, and division. Addition is the combination of two acts of counting into one act. The two acts of counting up to three and counting up to six are done as one act when one adds three and six. The two acts are done immediately one after the other. We count to three and then count six more, reaching nine. Multiplication arises in a similar way.

One can always add two numbers or multiply two numbers and get an answer. For example, consider the counting numbers or integers like 1, 2, 3, 4, 5, etc., which are the ones we start with. If we add two counting numbers, the answer is a counting number. An example is $9 + 5 = 14$. Or if we multiply two integers, we get an integer as an answer, such a $9 \times 5 = 45$. This, however, does not always happen with subtraction or division. Nine minus seven ($9 - 7$) gives us the integer 2, but seven minus nine ($7-9$) does not give us an integer or counting number. Eight divided by two gives us the integer 4. But two divided by eight does not result in an integer.

These limitations in subtraction and division were the real reasons for new creative acts like the creative act resulting in counting numbers. The limitations in subtraction led to the creation of negative integers like -1, -2, -3. These are not useful in counting. Instead they make it possible that every two integers can be subtracted from one another and the answer is another integer. Now we can have 7 - 9 = -2. The same steps resulted in the creation of fractional numbers. These numbers permit us to divide any two integers and get an answer. Two divided by eight gives us 2/8 or 1/4 which, though not an integer, is another created number, a fractional number.

The integers, positive and negative, and the fractional numbers, positive and negative, are collected together as what are called rational numbers. This step is a new creative act of the human mind. In the system of rational numbers we have a tool of far greater perfection than in the counting numbers though both are equally the result of creative acts.

Notes *(while reading)*

Opening question *(after reading)*

Comments *(after discussion)*

6.   *Leviathan,*
by T. Hobbes

    Nature has made men roughly equal in body and mind. When everything is considered, the difference between one man and another is not very great. The case of bodily strength serves as a good example. The weakest man has enough strength to kill the strongest. He can do this either by some trick or by using a weapon or by joining with other men. The same is true of men's minds. Inequalities can be made up by various means.

    This rough equality in ability produces in every man the equal hope of getting what he wants. So when two men desire something which only one can have, this equality encourages both to strive for it. They therefore become enemies. Each man tries to destroy or defeat the other in order to get what he needs to keep alive or to enjoy his life. If we consider what men are like when they do not live in societies, we find that they become enemies. When one defeats the other, the victor must, in turn, expect a third person to try to take away what he has won.

    So it is clear what men are like when there is no outside power to keep them all in fear. Such a state of nature becomes a condition of war. In such a war every man struggles with every other man. War does not only mean constant fighting. A period of time during which a willingness to fight is commonly known and accepted is also called war.

    So in the state of nature, every man is every other man's enemy. There is no safety or security except one's own strength and trickery. In this state of things there can be no factories or stores because products are always unsafe. There can be no farming, no trading, no large buildings, no arts, no sciences, no society. Worst of all there would be continual fear and danger of violent death. The life of man would be solitary, poor, nasty, brutish and short.

This state of nature might not actually have existed and I certainly do not believe it existed throughout the world. Yet if we look at what men are now like in societies, we can convince ourselves how men would be in a purely natural condition. At night we all lock our houses and when we walk the streets we are constantly on guard. This shows that we believe that only fear of an outside power keeps men in check Nations and kings who have nothing to fear act toward one another just as we describe individual men acting in a state of nature. When a peaceful society falls into civil war we see what men are really like outside of society.

Notes *(while reading)*

Opening question *(after reading)*

Comments *(after discussion)*

Adam and Eve made love. She became pregnant and gave birth to Cain. She said, "I've had a baby with the help of the Lord." Later she gave birth to Cain's brother Abel. Abel became a shepherd and Cain became a farmer. In the course of time, Cain and Abel brought offerings to the Lord. Cain brought the fruits of the ground. Abel offered the firstborn of his flock. The Lord accepted Abel and his offering. However, for Cain and his offering he showed no favor. Cain became very angry. The Lord said to Cain, "Why are you angry? If you do well, will you not be accepted? And if you don't do well, sin is crouching for you at the door like a beast; it hungers for you, but you can win out over it."

Cain said to his brother Abel, "Let's go out to the fields." And when they were out in the fields Cain attacked his brother Abel and killed him. Soon after, the Lord said to Cain, "Where is your brother Abel?" And Cain answered, "How should I know? Am I my brother's keeper?" And the Lord said, "What have you done? Your brother's blood is crying out to me from the ground. And you are cursed from this ground which opened its mouth to receive your brother's blood from your own hand. When you dig the ground, it will no longer flourish or produce its fruits for you. You shall be a wanderer on the earth."

Notes *(while reading)*

Opening question *(after reading)*

Comments *(after discussion)*

8.   *Discourse on Method,*
by R. Descartes

I don't know if I should tell you about my most serious thoughts. This is because they are so philosophical and so strange that almost everyone would think I was wrong. But since I want you to be able to judge if what I have said and will say is right, I must tell you about them.

For a long time I had noticed that in everyday life we follow opinions and beliefs which we are unsure about. In fact, we follow them as if we couldn't doubt them at all. But what I am now doing is completely different from everyday life. I don't plan to do anything; instead, I plan to spend my time looking for the truth about all things. Therefore it appeared best to take the opposite approach. If any belief seemed at all able to be doubted, I would pretend that it is false. This way I might find a belief which could not, however hard I tried, be doubted at all.

First, I considered our senses. Because our eyes and ears sometimes tricked us I decided to pretend our senses were always wrong. Second, I thought about proofs and arguments. I remembered that people sometimes make mistakes about the simplest reasoning in geometry. And since I make mistakes as often as anyone else, I thought I should doubt all the proofs I used to accept. Third, I considered dreams. Since I have had the same ideas in dreams as when awake, I decided to suppose my waking ideas as false as my sleeping ones.

So I got very far in doubting all things. But as I made this strange effort, I noticed one important matter. It was necessary that the **I**, who doubted or thought these thoughts, should be something. I noticed that this truth, "I think therefore I am" was so certain that I couldn't even imagine a way to doubt it as in the other three cases. I therefore decided to accept it as true. In fact, I accepted it as the most certain truth and tried to build all the other truths on this foundation.

Notes *(while reading)*

Opening question *(after reading)*

Comments *(after discussion)*

9. *The Prince*, Ch. XV,
by N. Machiavelli

I wish now to speak about how a ruler should treat his friends and subjects. Many famous authors have written about this, and I am afraid you will think that I am being arrogant for writing about it again. This is especially so since what I have to say is so different from what the famous authors of the past have said. They have written about imaginary governments which don't exist in reality. To me it seems more useful to write down the simple truth of the matter.

There is such a great difference between how human beings actually live, and how they ought to live. A ruler who ignores what is *being* done by human beings in order to think about what *ought* to be done will bring about his own destruction. Since a ruler always has subjects who are not good, he too must *learn* how not to be good.

Let us therefore stop talking about imaginary things and start saying what is true about a ruler. All men, rulers included, are said to have qualities for which they are praised and blamed. Some men are called generous, others stingy, some cruel, other merciful, some treacherous, others faithful, some cowardly, others brave, some religious, others unreligious, and so on.

Everyone will agree that it would be nice if a ruler had all the qualities mentioned above that are considered good. However, it is impossible to have them all, for human nature is not like that. The ruler should be smart enough not to get the reputation for having those bad qualities which could cause him to lose power. As for the other bad qualities, he should not worry too much about his reputation. If he thinks about the matter carefully he will see that if he tries to acquire certain qualities which seem good he might lose his power. On the other hand, some other qualities which seem bad will help him to increase his power.

Notes *(while reading)*

Opening question *(after reading)*

Comments *(after discussion)*

10.   *Mathematical Principles,*
by I. Newton

Laws of Motion

Law A

A body which is either at rest or in motion with constant speed in a straight line stays that way. It changes its speed or direction only when forced to do so by something else.

If you throw something it will keep on moving at constant speed in a straight line. However, all bodies are slowed down by air resistance, or pulled downward by the force of gravity. A top would not stop spinning if it were not slowed down by moving through the air. Planets and comets are much bigger and move through space in which there is very little air resistance. They therefore keep their motions, both circular and in a straight line, for a much longer time.

Law B

To every action there is always opposed an equal reaction. That is, when two bodies act on one another, these actions are equal but in opposite directions.

A body which pushes or pulls another body is pushed by that other just as much. If you press a stone with your finger, your finger is also pressed by the stone. If a horse pulls a stone tied to a rope, the horse (if I may say so) will be pulled back toward the stone just as much. This is because the rope which is being stretched pulls the horse toward the stone as much as the stone toward the horse.

29

Notes (while reading)

Opening question (after reading)

Comments (after discussion)

11. _The Confessions,_ Bk. II,
by St. Augustine

God, your law punishes theft. This law is written in our hearts and no amount of evil or crime can erase it. We can see this because no thief, not even a rich one, will let another man, even one who is very poor, steal from him. Yet, I both wanted to steal and did steal. And what is so surprising, I was not forced to do it by needing anything. I stole something which I already had. I stole pears, though I already had pears which were better than the ones I took. I had no wish to eat what I stole. What I enjoyed was stealing itself.

Near my parent's garden was a neighbor's pear tree. Though it was loaded with fruit, the pears looked rotten. I and some friends got the idea of shaking the pears off the tree and carrying them away. We set out late at night and stole all the fruit we could carry. We tasted a few and then threw the rest to the pigs. The pleasure we felt was simply in doing something which was forbidden. We took no pleasure in eating the pears, nor in being out late at night.

Notes *(while reading)*

Opening question *(after reading)*

Comments *(after discussion)*

12.   *The Physics,* Bk. II, Ch. 8,
by Aristotle

Some serious people say that nature does not have purposes. That is, that nature does not work for goals. They say that things happen because hot is hot, and cold is cold. For example, rain doesn't come so that corn will grow and people will eat and prosper. Rather, it rains because water, heated by the sun, rises from the earth by evaporation and then, chilled by the atmosphere, becomes water again and falls as rain. Sometimes that is good for a farmer; sometimes it is not.

They make the same claim about each living thing. It just so happens, they say, that the teeth that are good for cutting are in the front of our mouths, and the teeth that are good for grinding what has already been cut are at the back of our mouths. It turns out well, but why should we think there is any purpose in it? After all, mere coincidence or chance might have brought about this arrangement of teeth in some living thing, and because of this the living thing was able to survive. This, however, is a bad argument. Mere coincidence or chance is not like that. What happens always, or almost always is not a matter of coincidence. It is a matter of how things naturally are.

Yet, many people wonder how nature can have purposes. They say that there is a great difference between the way human beings make things, and what happens naturally. They admit that when a carpenter makes a table, he has a purpose in mind. But oak trees, they say, just grow.

This opinion does not make sense. When I make something, I desire, and I choose, and I arrange things. Now think of a bird's nest, or a spider's web. If I were making those things would I make them differently? How do plants know to grow their roots down rather than up in order to find food?

Don't worry because you don't see birds, spiders and plants trying to choose. Sometimes the goal and the choice are not separate from what happens. If nature wanted to make boats, it would make them the same way we make them. The maker doesn't have to be separate from the thing made. Think of a doctor doctoring himself. Nature is like that.

Notes (while reading)

Opening question (after reading)

Comments (after discussion)

13.   *The Elements*, Bk. I,
by Euclid

Definitions

1.   A **point** is that which has no parts.
2.   A **line** is length without thickness.
3.   The ends of a line are **points**.

---

4.   An **angle** is the inclination to one another of two lines which meet and do not lie in a straight line. In the figure, the angles formed by the straight lines AB and DC are angle ABC and angle ABD.

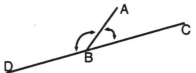

5.   Suppose two lines meet and form angles. If the angles next to one another are equal, the angles are called **right angles**. In the figure, angle ABC equals angle ABD. These are therefore called right angles.

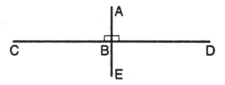

6.   **Parallel straight lines** are straight lines which, extended to any length in both directions, do not meet in either direction.

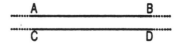

Postulates

1. A straight line can be drawn from any point to any other point.

2. A limited straight line can be produced continuously in a straight line.

3. A circle with any point as center and any size radius can be drawn.

4. All right angles are equal to one another.

5. Suppose the straight line AB falls on the two straight lines AD and BC. Suppose also that the two angles DAB and ABC added together are less than two right angles. Then the straight lines AD and BC, when produced at D and C, will meet in that direction.

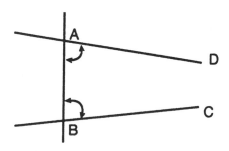

Notes *(while reading)*

Opening question *(after reading)*

Comments *(after discussion)*

14.   *Pensées,*
by B. Pascal

    Even as children we are told to take care of our reputations, our property, and our friends. We are even told to look after the reputations and property of our friends. We are given chores and homework, and are constantly told that we will not be happy unless both we and our friends have health, good reputations, and money in the bank. If one thing goes wrong, we are told we will be unhappy. So, from the first moment of each day we are burdened with responsibilities.

    You will say that this is a strange way to make people happy. Could one even imagine a better way to make them unhappy? But what should one do? If you took people's worries away they would be forced to look at themselves. They would have to think about what they are, where they come from, and where they are going. For many, these thoughts would be unbearable. This is why people have to keep busy. Even when they have free time, they are advised to spend it keeping busy with sports and hobbies. Isn't such a person's heart empty and ugly?

Notes *(while reading)*

Opening question *(after reading)*

Comments *(after discussion)*

Then Jesus told another story. He said that there was a man who had two sons. The younger son said to his father, "Give me my fair share of your property now. Give it to me in cash." His father did this. A few days later the son left home and went to a country that was far away. There he wasted all his money on having a good time. Then there was a famine in that land and people were hungry, and he was hungry too. So he got a job on a farm feeding pigs. He was paid very little. He sometimes thought he would be better off eating what the pigs ate rather than what he could afford to eat. But he was too proud to eat what the pigs were eating.

Then he came to his senses. He said to himself, "The people who work for my father eat well, and I am starving. I will leave this place and go to my father and say, 'Father, I have sinned against heaven and against you. I no longer deserve to be called your son. Please treat me like one of your workers.'" So he left that place and went back to his father.

While he was still a long way off, his father saw him coming. His father was old and dignified. His father was moved to see him, and ran to him and embraced him and kissed him. The son said, "I have sinned against heaven and against you. I no longer deserve to be called your son." But his father interrupted him and said to the servants, "Quick, bring out the most beautiful clothing, and put it on my son. And prepare a wonderful dinner—I don't care about the cost. We are going to celebrate. This son of mine was dead, and he has come back to life. He was lost and now he is found." And so they began to celebrate.

The older brother was out in the fields, hard at work. He started on his way home and as he drew near, he heard the sounds of a party. He asked one of the servants what was happening. The servant said, "Your brother has come home and your father is celebrating because his son is safe and sound."

The older brother became angry, and refused to go into the house. His father came out to invite him. The older brother said, "This isn't fair. For many years I worked for you and I never disobeyed you, but you never gave a party for me. But this son of yours comes back having spent all your money—he and his women friends—and you have a celebration for him. It isn't fair."

The father said, "My son, you are always with me, and all that I have is yours. But it is right that we should be happy and celebrate, because your brother here was dead and has come to life. He was lost and now he is found."

Notes *(while reading)*

Opening question *(after reading)*

Comments (after discussion)

16. *The Philosophy of History,*
by G.W.F. Hegel

We see changes in history. These are often described as an advance to something better or more perfect. We also see changes in nature. These, however, only show us a cycle which always repeats itself. About nature, people often say that there is nothing new under the sun. The changes in nature cause a feeling of boredom. Only in the region of the human spirit—history—do they say that anything new arises. History and nature are different. This has convinced some thinkers that man has a different destiny from natural objects like stones, planets, trees, and animals. Natural objects have a stable character in spite of the changes that occur to them. Among human beings, however, there appears a real capacity for change for the better. In other words, among humans there is what has been called an impulse of perfectibility. Some claim that human beings can become better and better without end.

The principle of perfectibility gives historical changes a definite order. Certain nations and religions have rejected this idea of change for the better. These countries claim that their system of government is already perfect. Many religions believe they already possess the truth. These countries and religions insist that they must be outside the law of perfectibility. One can understand why they make that claim. But let's assume that changes in our world are not accidental. Then these countries and religions can no longer explain the destruction of government or religion by the silliness of men or by their evil passions, both of which are accidental occurrences.

Many people think they notice this principle of

perfectibility in history. I think it is almost as vague an idea as natural change itself. For the principle does not state a purpose or a goal or a standard. The improved or more perfect state of things is never defined. It is entirely left up in the air. I claim that if nature and human history are different, a better account of their differences must be given.

Notes *(while reading)*

Opening question *(after reading)*

Comments *(after discussion)*

17.   *The Pessimist's Handbook,*
by A. Schopenhauer

A man's happiness and also almost every friendship he has both rest on illusion. As a rule when he learns more about either, the happiness or friendship disappears. In spite of this, here as everywhere, people must have courage and pursue truth. They must never get tired of trying to get straight about themselves and the world. When they discover that an illusion made them happy, they should have courage and keep moving ahead. People who do this can be certain of one thing. They will never discover any worthlessness in themselves. For to feel one is worthless is the worst and in fact the only suffering.

All sufferings of the mind are healed, and in fact, immediately relieved, by the firm sense of one's own worth. A person who believes in his worth can sit down quietly under the weight of terrible sufferings. Though such a person may have no pleasures, no joys, and no friends, he can rest content in himself. That's how strong a comfort can come from feeling one's own worth. It is the greatest blessing on earth. On the other hand, nothing can help a person who knows his own worthlessness. All he can do is try to hide it by deceiving other people. Or he can try to deafen them by making lots of noise. Unfortunately, neither trick can serve him for very long.

Notes *(while reading)*

Opening question *(after reading)*

Comments *(after discussion)*

18.   *Introduction to Experimental Medicine,*
by C. Bernard

Do we have the right to experiment on animals? As for me, I think we definitely have this right. It would be strange if we said that human beings have the right to use animals for food, but don't have the right to use them for learning things which are useful for preserving human life. You cannot deny that progress in medicine needs experiments. We can save some living beings from death only by killing others. Experiments must be made, either on human beings or on animals. If it is wrong to do experiments on human beings, then it must be right to do experiments on animals. This is true even if the experiments are painful and dangerous to the animal, as long as they are useful to human beings.

What about the objections of some serious people who are not scientists? They feel that experiments on animals are wrong because the animals suffer. They think the scientists who do these experiments are cruel. But what about a soldier who has to kill for his country, or a surgeon who must hurt someone in order to cure him? Are they also cruel? Are they like a person who likes to hurt other people? I don't think so! What makes them different is the ideas they have. The doctor wants to cure disease.   The soldier wants to protect his country.   In the same way the medical scientist who does experiments on living animals wants to learn things. He is following his own scientific idea. He doesn't hear the cries of the animals or see the blood which is flowing. What other people find disgusting he finds interesting. As long as he is under the influence of the scientific idea nothing else matters very much to him. People who don't share his idea will think that he is cruel, and he won't be able to convince them that he isn't. He will be able to discuss what he does only with other scientists. Only his own conscience can tell him whether what he is doing is right or wrong.

Notes *(while reading)*

Opening question *(after reading)*

Comments *(after discussion)*

19.   *The Republic*, Bk. II,
by Plato

Do people behave justly because they want to? Or are
they just and fair because they are afraid to be unjust? To
answer these questions let us pretend we can give both the just
and unjust man the freedom and power to do whatever they
please.   Then in our imaginations we can see where their
desires will lead them. The just person will be no different
from the unjust person. For he looks to what is to his self-
interest just as much as the unjust man does. Only fear of the
law makes him just. Let me tell you a story about a man who
had such freedom.

People say that he was a shepherd in the service of the
king of Lydia. After a great rainstorm and an earthquake, the
ground opened up where he was caring for sheep, and he went
into the opening in the earth. The story goes on to say that he
saw many marvels there, among which was a hollow bronze
horse with little doors. When he peeped in, he saw the body
of a giant with a gold ring on its hand. He took the ring and
left.

When the shepherds held their monthly meeting to
report to the king about his flocks, he also attended, wearing
the ring. While he was sitting there twisting the ring on his
finger, he happened to turn it so that the stone faced his palm.
When he did this, the story goes on, he became invisible to
those who sat around him. They spoke about him as if he were
not there. He was amazed, and fumbled with his ring. When
he turned the stone out, he became visible again. He tested
this many times, and found that the ring really possessed this
power of making him invisible when he wanted. So with the
help of this ring, he seduced the king's wife, and got her to
help him kill the king and take over his kingdom.

Now suppose we have two such rings. Let's give one to a just man and the other to an unjust man. It is hard to believe that even a just man would stop himself from stealing if he knew he would never get caught.

Notes *(while reading)*

Opening question *(after reading)*

Comments *(after discussion)*

20. *The Motion of Colliding Bodies,*
by C. Huygens

Hypothesis I: Any body already in motion continues to move forever with the same speed, and in a straight line, unless it is interfered with.

Hypothesis II: Let us suppose that two identical bodies travelling at the same speed collide with one another. After the collision each rebounds with the same speed it had before the collision.

Hypothesis III: The speed of a body is always determined in relation to other bodies which we consider to be at rest. However, the body whose speed we are trying to determine and the bodies which we consider to be at rest could all in addition have a common motion. Since this additional motion is common to all the bodies, it doesn't affect any of our conclusions. This means that if we allow two bodies to collide, and, in addition to their motion toward one another, they both share a common motion, the result is the same as if that common motion were totally absent.

For example, let someone who is on a boat moving with constant speed make two equal balls which are moving with equal speeds collide with one another. The equal speeds of the balls are determined by this person in relation to himself. He considers himself to be at rest. According to Hypothesis II, the balls will rebound with equal speeds. It is as if he had done the experiment while standing in a motionless boat or on the ground instead of in the moving boat. The moving boat, since it moves the observer and both balls equally, drops out of the picture.

Notes *(while reading)*

Opening question *(after reading)*

Comments (after discussion)

21.   *Passers-by,*
by F. Kafka

When you go walking at night up a street and a man, visible a long way off—for the street goes uphill and there is a full moon—comes running toward you, well, you don't catch hold of him as he passes. You let him run on even if he is a feeble old man, even if someone is chasing him and yelling at him.

For it is night, and you can't help it if the street goes uphill in the moonlight. And besides, these two have maybe started the chase to amuse themselves, or perhaps they are both chasing a third person, or perhaps the first is an innocent man and the second wants to murder him and so you would become an accessory, or they are merely running separately home to bed, or perhaps the first has a gun.

And anyhow, haven't you a right to be tired, haven't you been drinking a lot of wine? You're thankful they are now both long out of sight.

Notes *(while reading)*

Opening question *(after reading)*

Comments *(after discussion)*

22. *The Proslogium,*
by St. Anselm

Lord, you give understanding about what you are to those who believe in you. So let me understand that you are just what I believe you are. I believe that you are the greatest thing we can think of. But though this is what I believe about you, perhaps there is in fact no such thing as you. For aren't there some foolish people who say that God does not exist, and can't they be right? Yet even these fools understand me when I speak about you. They understand this about you: that you are the greatest thing we can think of. That's what we mean by God. What the foolish person understands is at least in his thought. However, he does not think that you exist in the world. Let me make this difference clear.

It is one thing for an object to be in thought. It is quite another thing to understand that an object exists. Take the case of a painter. At first he thinks of what he will later paint. At that stage he has it in his thought. But he knows it does not yet exist because he has not painted it. After he has made the painting, the object exists in both ways. He has it in his thought, and he understands that it exists. Let us now see, God, if this difference applies to you, too. If it does the fool would be right.

As I said, even the foolish person is convinced that God at least exists in thought. For when he hears me talk about the greatest thing we can think of, that is, God, he understands what I say. And where else can what we understand exist if it is not in our thoughts? But I say that this particular thing—God—can not exist only in thought. For can't we at least think him to exist also in the world? But what has happened? We have thought of an object which is greater than the object which was only in our thought. We have just thought of God existing both in our thought and in the world. Such a being obviously is greater than a God who only exists in our thought. We have, then, thought of a thing greater than the greatest thing. So the greatest thing we can think of must exist both in thought and in reality. This greatest thing we can think of is you, God. You therefore exist both in our thought and in the world. The foolish people are wrong to think you don't exist. Thank you for helping me to understand what I already believe.

Notes *(while reading)*

Opening question *(after reading)*

Comments (after discussion)

by Euclid

Proposition 1: On a given straight line to construct a triangle with all the sides equal to each other.

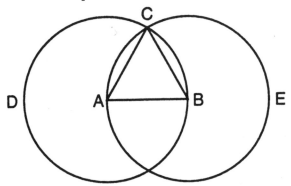

Let AB be the given straight line. We wish to construct an equilateral triangle on AB. Draw circle DCB with center A and radius AB. Again, with center B and radius BA, let circle ACE be drawn. From point C where the circles cut one another, draw straight lines AC and BC to the points A & B. Now, since point A is the center of the circle DCB, AC is equal to AB. This is because on a circle all points are the same distance from the center. Again, since point B is the center of the circle ACE, BC is equal to AB. But AC was also proved equal to AB.

Therefore each of the straight lines AC and BC is equal to AB. Since things which are equal to the same thing are equal to each other, AC is also equal to BC. The three lines AC, AB, and BC are therefore equal to one another. But, these three lines form a triangle. Therefore the triangle ABC has three equal sides, that is, is equilateral, and has been constructed on the line AB. That is what was to be done.

Notes *(while reading)*

Opening question *(after reading)*

Comments *(after discussion)*

24.   *The Metaphysics, Bk. I,*
by Aristotle

All human beings naturally want to know. A sign of this is that we like to use our senses; to see and hear and smell and touch and taste. We like to use our senses even when we are not using them to do something else. But, most of all, we like to see. Even when there is nothing we plan to do we enjoy seeing almost more than anything else. This is because seeing, most of all, makes us know that one thing differs from another, and that things have parts.

All animals are born with the ability to sense. In addition to this, some kinds of animals are able to remember. Other kinds are not able to remember. The ones that are able to remember are also able to learn.

So some animals live by sense experience and memory, but have only a small share in what we call *real* experience. Only the human animal has real experience, since only human beings are able to make many memories into one connected experience. There is what we might call experience or skill or know-how, and there is also what we might call art or knowledge. Experience makes us know that when Mary had this illness and when John had that illness, the same kind of treatment cured both of them. But only art or knowledge makes us know generally that anybody with an illness of a certain *kind* can be cured by a certain *kind* of treatment. Art and knowledge are impossible without experience. But art and knowledge make us know more than experience does. They make us know about relations between kinds of things, or *classes* of things. Experience only teaches about relations between *particular* things.

Another way of stating this difference is to say that in

64

experience we do not know *causes*, while through art and knowledge we do know *causes*.

So there is sensing, then remembering, then having a connected experience, and then having art and knowledge. When we have art and knowledge, we know about *kinds* of things, and about *causes*.

Notes *(while reading)*

Opening question *(after reading)*

Comments *(after discussion)*

25. _The Confessions_, Bk. X,
by St. Augustine

Music holds an important place in my heart. Yet sometimes it seems to me that I give it more importance than is right. I know that when holy words are sung well our minds are stirred up to a burning religious feeling. We then experience a much deeper flame of devotion than when these words are just spoken. However, our emotions are of many different kinds. By some secret link each emotion is stirred up by a certain type of song. Often I'm tricked by this fact. I receive pleasure from holy songs which my mind or soul should not feel. In church we should only feel the pleasures which our reason allows. Unfortunately, instead of following behind reason, our desire for pleasure often tries to take the lead. In the case of holy music I sin without realizing it. After the singing has stopped I often recognize that it was my body and not my soul which was pleased.

When I worry about being tricked in this way, I fall into the error of being too strict. At those times I want all music banished from the church. The safer course, then, appears to be what a famous bishop of Alexandria once suggested. A reader of Psalms, he said, should use so little change of voice that the effort is more like speaking than singing. But then I remember the tears I used to shed in church when Psalms were sung. This was just at the time when I was beginning to recover my faith. And I know that now I am often moved by the words sung and not by the singing. Once again, I see how important music can be. So I am sometimes convinced by the danger of the pleasure, and other times persuaded by the good that can be done. On the whole, I am inclined to favor singing in church. My hope is that the delight in pleasing sounds will stir weaker minds to a feeling of devotion. Yet for me, even now, the danger is still there. Whenever I am more moved by the singing than by the words, I think it would be better for me not to hear the music.

Notes (while reading)

Opening question (after reading)

Comments (after discussion)

26.   *The Will to Believe,*
by W. James

A religious person believes that the more perfect and more eternal aspect of the universe has a personal form. Religions call this aspect, or part, "God". A religious person cannot believe that the entire universe is a mere thing. Rather, part of the universe is a sort of person, a "Thou", God. Furthermore, religions hold that any relation that may be possible from person to person might also be possible here. We all recognize that we are in part passive portions of the universe, and that some things just happen to us. However, we also believe that we ourselves can take the first step and do things. This belief leads to the possibility that religion asks us to use our ability to take the first step. It might be that evidence for religious beliefs is withheld unless we meet it halfway.

Let me give an example. Imagine a person who was in the habit of going to the same club everyday. While there, he never greeted anyone first. Whenever anyone told him something, he never believed it without proof. He even went so far as to ask for everything in writing. How would other people respond to him? Don't you think that he would miss out on the pleasures of friendship he would have had if he had been more trusting? I believe that the universe might be like that. If we go around always asking for proof of God's existence, we might never get to know him at all if he exists. To get any evidence at all of God's existence, we might have to take the first step.

Notes (while reading)

Opening question (after reading)

Comments (after discussion)

27. *The Peloponnesian Wars,*
by Thucydides

Athens and Sparta, the two most powerful cities in Greece, had been at war with one another for many years. Athens, a great naval power, controlled most of the islands in the Aegean Sea. It was creating an empire, but some of the islands were not eager to join. One such island was Melos, which had been colonized by Sparta and wished to remain neutral. In the sixteenth year of the war, an Athenian fleet sailed to the island of Melos. As soon as the Athenian army landed, they sent ambassadors to negotiate with the most important men on the island.

Athenians: We don't plan to pretend we have a right to be on your island. In return, don't you bother telling us you won't join our enemies, the Spartans, or that you've never hurt us. All these claims would only hide the real issue. We both know the way the world is. Right and wrong come into play only between people whose power is equal. Otherwise, the strong do what they can. The weak suffer whatever is necessary.

Melians: You tell us to forget what is right and only consider what is in our self-interest. Agreed! Even so, it couldn't be useful to anyone—us or you—to deny us a privilege always allowed those in great danger. When someone is threatened, he is permitted to bring up what is fair and right. At those times, one is even allowed to use arguments which aren't quite logical if he can get them accepted. You Athenians should want to protect this custom too. You'll need it if you're ever defeated. For people will avenge themselves on you.

Ath: We're not afraid of the end of our empire. What is worse is subjects who attack and overpower their rulers. We're here, therefore, for the present interests of our empire. We want to rule you for the good of us both.

Mel: We'd love to hear how it's as good for us to serve you as for you to rule us.

Ath: You would gain by not being destroyed. We would gain by not destroying you.

Mel: So we can't be neutral.

Ath: No. Your hostility can't hurt us much. But to our subjects, your neutrality may look like our weakness.

Mel: But we're not in the same category as your subjects. They are either your colonists or those who have rebelled against you. We're neither.

Ath: To our subjects, there are only two kinds of people. There are those we rule and those we don't rule. And our subjects believe if we don't rule a people, it is because they're strong. If we don't attack them, it is because we are afraid. You're weaker than many of our subjects. We can't let you escape the masters of the sea.

Mel: All right. You won't let us talk about justice. We'll talk about self-interest. Our interests and yours are the same. Many cities and islands are still neutral. If you attack us, they'll think they're next. So they'll become your enemies even though they wouldn't have thought of doing so.

Ath: Neutrals on land don't concern us. It's the islanders like you and our discontented subjects who worry us. Both could take rash steps and lead themselves and us into danger.

Mel: If your subjects will risk so much to be free of you, how can you expect us to submit to you? We're still free. Shouldn't we try everything to avoid losing that?

Ath: If honor and shame were at stake, then perhaps you should. But they're not at issue because we're so much stronger than you. All you have to worry about is simply how to preserve yourselves.

Mel: Anything can happen in war. Numbers aren't always the crucial thing. If we give up, we have no hope. If we fight, there's still a chance.

Ath: Hope is very dangerous. Only those who have something to spare, something extra, can afford to hope. Hope can tempt us to absurd actions. We only recognize how flimsy our hope was when we are ruined. You are weak. Your survival hangs on a single throw of the dice. You can't risk hope. That's the way to destruction.

Mel: We know you are stronger. But we trust in the help of the gods since we are just men fighting against unjust men.

Ath: We have gods too. And there is a law that gods and men rule wherever they can. We didn't create this law. It was here before us. It will still exist after us. We act by it knowing that you, having our power, would do the same.

The Melians and Athenians then went to war. After a hard fight, Athens won. The Athenians killed all the Melian men. They sold the women and children into slavery.

Notes *(while reading)*

Opening question *(after reading)*

Comments (after discussion)

28.   *The Origin of Species,*
by C. Darwin

It has been said that all animals, and even plants, must struggle with one another in order to live. Nothing is easier than to admit this in words. Nothing is harder than to keep it constantly in mind. Yet, if we don't keep it in mind, we will misunderstand most of the things we see when we look at nature. At first glance, the face of nature is bright with gladness. We forget that the birds which are singing around us live on insects and seeds. They are constantly destroying life. We also forget that these birds and their eggs are themselves being destroyed by other birds and animals. One year there seems to be plenty of food. The next year there is starvation.

People have said that connections of all the living beings on earth to one another can be represented by a great tree. Let us consider the relation between this peaceful-looking tree and the struggle for life. The green and budding twigs represent the kinds of living things we see around us now. The green and budding twigs from previous years represent those kinds of animals and plants, like the saber-toothed tiger, which used to exist, and don't any more. All the growing twigs compete with one another for light just as kinds of animals compete with one another in the great battle for life. The big branches of the tree which were once small budding twigs now give rise to other branches. In the same way, animals which once lived and roamed the earth, and do so no more, have given rise to others until we come to the animals living today.

Of the many twigs which grew when the tree was small, only two or three survive. These are the biggest branches of the tree. From them all the other branches arise. So it is with animals which lived long ago. Very few of them have living descendants. They are known to us only from their bones which are buried in the earth. The buds on the tree give rise to other buds and the stronger branches cut off the light from the weaker ones and kill them. This is the great struggle for life in which only the strong survive and the weak perish. In the same way the Great Tree of Life fills the earth with its dead and broken branches and covers its surface with beautiful green buds.

Notes *(while reading)*

Opening question *(after reading)*

Comments *(after discussion)*

29. _A Mathematician's Defense,_
by G.H. Hardy

A mathematician, like a painter or a poet, is a maker of patterns. If his patterns are more permanent that theirs, it is because his are made with _ideas_. A painter makes patterns with shapes and colors, a poet with words. A mathematician, on the other hand, works only with ideas. So his patterns are likely to last longer, since ideas don't wear out as quickly as words.

The mathematician's patterns, like the painter's or the poet's, must be _beautiful_. Beauty is the first test. It may be very hard to define mathematical beauty, but that's just as true of beauty of any kind. We may not be able to say what makes a poem beautiful, but we recognize one when we read it.

A chess problem is genuine mathematics, but it is in some way "trivial" mathematics. However clever and complicated, however original and surprising the moves, there is something essential lacking. Chess problems are _unimportant_. The best mathematics is _serious_ as well as beautiful—"important" if you like, but "serious" is better.

I am not thinking of the "practical" consequences of mathematics. At present, I will say only that if a chess problem is, in the crude sense, "useless", then that is equally true of most of the best mathematics. Very little of mathematics is useful practically, and that little is dull. The "seriousness" of a mathematical theorem lies not in its practical consequences which are usually slight. Instead, the seriousness of a theorem lies in the significance of the mathematical ideas it connects together. We may say, roughly, that a mathematical idea is "significant" if it can be connected, in a natural way, with a large body of other mathematical ideas. By this means the theorem is likely to lead to advances in mathematics itself, and even in the other sciences.

Notes *(while reading)*

Opening question *(after reading)*

Comments (after discussion)

30.   *The Iliad*, Bk. XXII,
by Homer

In the tenth year of the war between the Greeks and the Trojans, the greatest Greek warrior, Achilles, killed the most courageous and strongest Trojan, Hector. Because Hector had killed Achilles' closest friend, the Greek was not satisfied by his enemy's death. For days, Achilles insulted Hector's dead body as the Trojan's father, King Priam, longing to recover his son's body for burial, remained helpless in his city. Each day, Achilles dragged Hector's dead body through the dust. At night he returned to his tent to rest, refusing to eat. This day was no different. He rested in his tent waiting for the dawn when he would continue his revenge against the dead man.

Suddenly Achilles saw a tall kingly old man before him. It was Priam, king of the Trojans, and father of Hector. Priam kneeled before the Greek and kissed the hands which had killed so many of his sons. "Achilles, remember your own father," Priam said. "He must be my age. Perhaps right now in a faraway country, people are causing him pain. But nothing he suffers can compare with my misery. He is happy knowing that you, his son, are still alive. I once had fifty sons, but now most are dead. Yet worst of all is the death of my best son, Hector. You killed him and now I come all alone into your camp to ask for his body. Take pity on me. Remember your own father. For I am more to be pitied than any man alive. What other man has had to come through great danger to kiss the hand of his son's killer?"

Priam's words stirred in Achilles a great sadness for his own father. He pushed the old man's hands away gently. Priam sat on the floor. Achilles remained on the stool. They sat near one another, each remembering those who were not there. Priam wept for his dead son, Hector. Achilles, looking at Priam's face, wept for his own absent father and for his dead friend. The young warrior and the old king wept together.

When the Greek had had enough of his grief, he got up from his chair. He took the old king's hand and raised him to his feet. "How could you have risked coming to my ships, old man? Your heart must be iron. Sit on this chair and you and I will end our grief. What's the use of weeping? We both know what everyone's life is like. A god, Zeus perhaps, has two jars. One holds good things, the other contains troubles and misery. Each person gets some of both. Sometimes one has good fortune. Other times one has bad fortune. This is how it was for my own father. He was a ruler of men, had riches and property and was given a goddess for a wife. Yet, he too received evil. Unlike you, he had only one son and I give him no help as he grows old. I sit here, far away, bringing pain and sorrow to you and your children. And you, Priam, once ruled this whole area with your sons. Now your kingdom must fight constantly and your sons are dead. Don't mourn endlessly. You can never bring Hector back to life."

"Achilles," said the old king. "Don't make me sit here while my dead son still lies in the dust. Please let me see him and take him home. The presents I've brought are valuable. Take them and give me my son."

Achilles frowned and stared at Priam. "Don't stir me up, old man! I give him back because I give him back. Don't remind me of my own grief or I may strike you even here in my tent."

Priam was frightened. The young Greek warrior, moving like a lion, left the tent. He took the ransom out of Priam's wagon and then went to find serving-maids. He ordered them to wash Hector's dead body. He did this because he was afraid Priam would break down at the sight of his son's dirty, broken body. The old man might be unable to hold back his anger. Achilles was afraid that this would remind him of his own grief and he would, there in his tent, kill the old man.

Achilles returned to his tent and spoke. "Priam, we must both eat. Even Niobe, whose twelve children were killed, ate when she was worn out with crying. Afterwards, you can take your son home to bury him."

The two men ate. These two men, who had wept and mourned together, now looked at one another. Each admired the other. Achilles appeared as a god to the old king. Priam appeared brave and dignified to the young warrior. The two men then slept. At dawn, Priam put his son on the wagon and took him home to bury him and to prepare his people to fight again.

Notes *(while reading)*

Opening question *(after reading)*

Comments *(after discussion)*

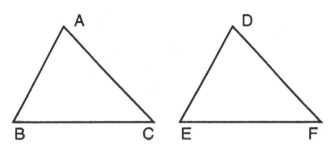

Let ABC and DEF be two triangles. Let side AB
equal side DE, and side AC equal side DF. In addition, let
angle BAC equal angle EDF.

I say that the third sides BC and EF are equal to one
another. I also say that the two triangles are equal. In
addition, angle ABC equals angle DEF, while angle ACB
equals angel DFE.

For, let triangle ABC be applied or placed on top of
triangle DEF. If point A is placed on point D, and straight line
AB is placed on DE, then point B coincides with point E.
This is because line AB equals line DE.

Since line AB coincides with line DE, line AC will
coincide with line DF. This is because we supposed that angle
BAC equals angle EDF. Point C will coincide with point F
since line AC is equal to line DF.

But point B also coincides with point E.

The third side of one triangle, the line BC, must then
coincide with the line EF, which is the third side of the second
triangle.

Since things which coincide are equal, the sides,
because they coincide, must be equal. We now have the three
sides of triangle ABC coinciding with the three sides of

triangle DEF.

The two triangles must coincide and so also be equal.

But then the remaining angles of triangle ABC will coincide with the remaining angles of triangle DEF.   Angle ABC coincides with angle DEF, and angle ACB coincides with angle DFE.

Since things which coincide are equal, these angles are equal to one another.

That is what it was required to prove.

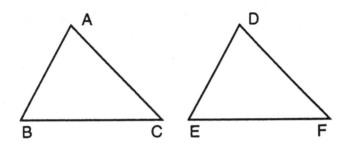

Notes *(while reading)*

Opening question *(after reading)*

Comments *(after discussion)*

32.   *The Prince*, Ch. XVII,
by N. Machiavelli

Is it better for a ruler to be loved by his people or feared by them? Most people want to be both feared and loved. However, it is hard to be both feared and loved, and if you can't have both, it is safer to be feared. This is so because human beings generally have the following characteristics: they are ungrateful, undependable, liars, cheats, cowards, and greedy for money. As long as you take care of them, they will do whatever you want. They will pretend they love you. They will offer to give you their property and their children, if they are sure you neither want them nor need them. If you ever do need them, they will turn against you. Since their friendship has been bought for a price, and does not depend on their goodness, you cannot count on it.

They will not hesitate to hurt their friends if they think they can profit by it. They will break the bonds of friendship every time they think it is in their interest to do so. However, they will not betray you if they fear you and think you can punish them. Although a ruler must make himself feared, he should not also make himself hated. It is, in fact, possible for a ruler to be feared but not hated. He can do this by keeping his hands off the women and property of his subjects. If he has to kill someone, he should do it when he can give a good reason for it. Anyway, most men will hate you more if you take their property than if you kill their friends and relatives.

Notes *(while reading)*

Opening question *(after reading)*

Comments *(after discussion)*

33. *The Apology,*
by Plato

(Meletus has accused Socrates of corrupting the young people in Athens. He has taken him to court. Socrates is defending himself.)

Socrates: Meletus, you think it's very important for young people to be exposed to the best possible influences, don't you?

Meletus: Of course.

Soc: Very well, then tell the court who it is that has the best influence on the young.

Mel: The laws.

Soc: That isn't what I asked. Please name the person who best knows the laws.

Mel: The members of the jury.

Soc: Do you mean that they can educate young people and make them better?

Mel: Yes I do.

Soc: How about all the spectators in this court? Are they also able to educate young people and make them better?

Mel: Yes they are.

Soc: Then what about the government officials? Do they also have a good influence on the young?

Mel: Yes they do.

Soc: Then, Meletus, according to you, everybody in Athens has a good influence on the young. Everybody except me. Is that what you mean?

Mel: Socrates, that is exactly what I mean.

Soc: Meletus, you have just shown that you have absolutely no interest in the education of young people.   You're pretending to be interested only because you're out to get me. Let me show you how I know. Do you think that everybody in this court is a good horse trainer? Of course you don't. Most people in this court would harm horses if they tried to train them. You know that horse-training is very difficult. Is educating young people any less difficult? Not very many people know how to do it. We Athenians would be very lucky if you were right. If only it were true that only one person had a bad influence on young people, and everyone else had a good influence. But we both know this isn't true. This is how I know you are not interested in young people at all, but are only out to get me. But, let's go on to something else. Is it better to live in a good community or in a bad one? In other words, is there anyone who would rather be harmed by his fellow citizens than benefitted by them? Answer me like a good fellow; the law says you must.

Mel: Of course not.

Soc: Well then, when you accuse me of trying to harm young people, do you mean that I do it on purpose or accidently?

Mel: On purpose.

Soc: Are you so much smarter than I am, Meletus? We have just agreed that it is better to live in a good community than in a bad one. Yet now you say that I am harming young people and thus making Athens worse. If you thought about it for even one minute you would see that no one would harm young people on purpose. He would only be harming himself. If I ever did harm young people, I did it accidently. It was because I failed as a teacher. If this is true you should have taken me aside and tried to persuade me to change. But you never did that. You never spoke to me until you got me in court. Now you want to punish me, not to teach me. This is how I know that you are not at all interested either in education or in young people.

Notes *(while reading)*

Opening question *(after reading)*

Comments (after discussion)

34.   *The Assayer*,
by Galileo

I cannot imagine a body which doesn't have a definite size and shape. I must also imagine it being in a particular place at some particular time. This body must either be in motion or at rest. It is either in contact with some other body, or alone. No matter how hard I try, I cannot separate my idea of a body from these conditions. However, I don't think the same is true of colors, tastes, sounds, and smells. I think that colors, tastes, sounds, and smells don't belong to the body at all, but are only in the eyes, tongue, ears, and nose of whoever observes the body. The observer could be a human being or some other animal. If there were no animals in the world, there wouldn't be colors, tastes, sounds, and smells. Yet, we ordinarily believe that these belong to a body as much as shape, size, position, time, and motion do. For example, don't we ordinarily believe that the color of a table belongs to it as much as its shape does? I think this is wrong.

I think I can explain what I mean better if I give an example. Suppose I move my hand first over a marble statue of a man and then over a living man. In both cases I am doing the same thing with my hand. I am moving my hand and touching the bodies at the same time. But when I touch the living man on the soles of his feet he says he is being tickled. Would you want to say that the hand had in itself the property of tickling? When I move my hand over the statue it surely isn't being tickled. Tickling belongs entirely to a living and sensing animal. If there were no animals in the world there would be no tickling. I believe the same is true about colors, tastes, sounds, and smells.

Notes *(while reading)*

Opening question *(after reading)*

Comments (after discussion)

35. *The Laws,*
by Hippocrates

1. Medicine is the noblest of the arts, but it has a bad reputation because many of those who practice it are not skilled. The reason for this is that bad doctors are not punished except by being disgraced. As we know, being disgraced does not hurt people who are used to it. Bad doctors are like statues which look like human beings, but are not alive. Many are called doctors, but in reality there are only few who really are.

2. If a person is to become a competent doctor, he must have the talent for medicine, a good education, willingness to work hard, and time and money to do it. If he doesn't have the talent, nothing else matters. If he does, then a good education can be profitable. However, he must be willing to work very hard if this education is to do him any good.

3. Education in medicine is like farming. Our talents are the soil; the words of our teachers are seed, and instruction to young people is like planting the seed in the ground at the right time. Hard work is like tending fields. It takes time to make things grow and mature, both vegetables and doctors.

4. If one does all this, then he will be a doctor in fact and not just in name. But, he also needs to get experience. A person without experience is either too timid, or too bold. This is because he has no self-confidence.

5. Medical knowledge is sacred, and should be given only to persons who deserve it. It should not be given to everyone.

Notes *(while reading)*

Opening question *(after reading)*

Comments (after discussion)

36.   *Mathematics as Creation,*
by H. Poincaré

How does it happen that there are people who do not follow mathematical arguments?   Most of us follow mathematical reasoning only with great difficulty, if we follow it at all.   This is very surprising when we think about it.   If mathematics only uses logical rules which are common to all normal minds, common to us all, how can we go wrong?   Why is mathematics so hard for most people?   A normal mind should not make logical mistakes, yet there are clever people with fine minds, who are unable to follow longer mathematical proofs.

There is one obvious answer which we must explore. Imagine a long series of short arguments, where the conclusion of the first little argument becomes the beginning of the second short argument, and so on to the twentieth or fiftieth short argument.   The mathematical conclusion is the end of the whole long argument.   We can all follow each little argument.   However, it is when we take the conclusion of one little argument and carry it on to the next argument that we either forget it a bit, or we don't quite understand it.   When it reappears at the beginning of the next argument, it is slightly different, or we give it a different meaning.

For these very same reasons I am a bad chess player. I see well enough that a certain move I thought of exposes me to danger.   Then I think of other moves I could take, and reject them one by one for equally clear reasons.   Finally, I make the move I first rejected because by that time I had forgotten the danger a few moves ahead.   Why is it then, that my memory is not good enough to make me a decent chess player?   My memory does not fail me when I'm doing a very difficult piece of mathematical reasoning that would be too hard for most chess players.

It is because a mathematical demonstration is not just a lot of little arguments strung together as a chess game is. It is little arguments *placed in a special order*, and the order is more important than each part of the whole demonstration. If I have the feeling —grasp the idea—so to speak, of this order, I see the pattern of the whole. I need not fear that I might forget one of the parts. Once I grasp the order or pattern of the whole argument, I can reconstruct any part I may have forgotten.

It seems to me, then, that, if I really demonstrate an argument in mathematics, it's as though I actually invented it myself. At least I can say this, that even if I am not gifted enough to create it myself, I myself reinvent it each time I demonstrate it.

Notes *(while reading)*

Opening question *(after reading)*

Comments *(after discussion)*

37. *The Metaphysic of Morals,*
by I. Kant

When we can, we should give to others who are in need. It's one of our duties. We also know there are many people who give because they enjoy giving and not because it's a duty. They are pleased when they can give to others. They act without any hidden purpose such as self-interest or because they want to feel important. They are just kind, decent people. I claim there is a great difference between kind people and those who give because it's their duty. Giving because it's our duty has moral value. The same action, when done simply from kindness, has no moral worth at all. When a kind person helps another, he is only doing what he wants to do. In this action he is no different from anyone doing what he wants.

Suppose we very much want to honor someone. If it turns out to be useful to the public and in agreement with duty, it is perfectly fine to do it. Our action should be praised and encouraged. But we shouldn't be esteemed or admired for what we did. Our action lacked a real moral support. The support for our action should have been our duty, whether we felt like honoring that person or not. In the example we just gave, we *wanted* to honor someone. It just turned out to have been the right thing to do.

Take the case of a philanthropist, someone who loves others and gives money, food or buildings to people he doesn't even know. Suppose that he feels great sorrow because of a personal loss. He no longer cares about the troubles of others because now he is so overwhelmed by his own. Yet, he is still rich and powerful enough to help others who need it. Suppose now that he tears himself away from his own pain. He gives money to others because it is his duty and not only as in the past, because he wanted to. Then, for the first time, his action will have real moral worth.

Take another example. Suppose there is a decent person who is coldhearted and indifferent to the suffering and pain of others. Suppose also that he is very patient when he suffers. In addition, he also expects that other people should be just like him in difficult times. Such a person would not be the worst creature produced by nature. But even though he is not the sort of person who naturally loves and cares for others, he would still have in himself something far better than natural kindness. Would he not have a source of action which would give him a worth far greater than what comes from being good-natured and kind? Yes, without any doubt! Every person, whatever that person is like, can possess a moral worth which is, without any comparison, the greatest possible. In the cases we have looked at, such a person can be loving and caring and generous towards others from duty rather than because he wants by natural feeling to be that way.

Notes *(while reading)*

Opening question *(after reading)*

Comments (after discussion)

38. *"Life of Pericles"*,
by Plutarch

Augustus Caesar, Emperor of Rome, once saw some wealthy foreigners fondly holding puppies in their arms. Shocked, he asked whether women in their country had stopped having children. By this remark, the emperor was criticizing people who spend their kindness and affection on animals instead of on their own kind. In a similar way we criticize those who misuse the natural love of inquiry and observation. Most people observe and listen to what isn't worth their attention. They neglect things which are excellent in themselves and which might do them some good.

Our outward senses, our eyes and ears, respond to whatever strikes them. But with our inward senses, our minds and souls, we can choose. We have the power to direct ourselves to what we decide. So it becomes our duty to study and observe the very best objects. These objects are not only worth thinking about, but may also improve us. It is similar to how it is with colors. A fresh and pleasant color stimulates and strengthens the sight. So a person should focus his mind on what pleases it, strengthens it, and attracts it to its own good and advantage. For the mind, such objects are acts of virtue. When people see them, or read about them, such actions produce in our minds an eagerness to imitate them or even to do better.

In most things or actions we like, we don't feel a desire to act in that same way. Many times, in fact, we may be pleased with an object but scorn the person who made it. This happens with things like perfumes, beautiful dyes, or delicious food. We enjoy the product, but feel superior to the maker. There is an interesting story about Alexander the Great which bears on this point. King Philip listened to his son Alexander playing the flute with great skill. The king enjoyed the piece but turned to his son and said, "Aren't you ashamed to play so well? A king should be able to enjoy music. He should not be able to play it."

Even with great works of art, something similar is true. No person looking at the great statue of Jupiter by the famous sculptor Phidias ever desired to become another Phidias. For it doesn't follow that if a work pleases us by its beauty, the person who made it deserves our admiration. That's why these things really bring no great gain to the viewers. For on seeing them we don't desire to do the same thing. But virtue and nobility and honor and goodness are quite different. Even the mere account or story of them can so affect our minds that we admire the actions and want to imitate those who did them. We long to possess and enjoy money, power, and expensive homes, but we ourselves want to act courageously and nobly. We can quickly see the difference between these two kinds of things. We are quite content to be given money and expensive goods by others. But we want others to experience virtuous acts from us. Actions of this kind and moral good itself provoke us to actions of our own.

Notes *(while reading)*

Opening question *(after reading)*

Comments *(after discussion)*

39. *The Ethics,*
by Aristotle

A man is thought to be great who thinks that he is worthy of great things, and *is* worthy of them. If a man thinks that he is worthy of great things but is not, then he is only a fool. Self-esteem is connected to greatness, and a great person knows he deserves to be honored by others.

A truly great man must be the best in every way. For example, it would be wrong for a great man to run from danger, or to do wrong to someone else.

The great man is mostly concerned with honors, but only if they are given by good men. He will despise honors given by men who are less good or bad, and honors given for petty reasons. He will not care much about wealth and power, and he won't be overjoyed at good luck, or depressed if things go bad. So you can see why great men are thought to be proud. But some men are proud without having a right to be. They are only imitating what great men are, but are not themselves really great.

The great man likes to give favors, but he is ashamed of receiving them. To give is the mark of a superior person, and to have a favor done to you is to be inferior. The great man will forget or ignore favors done to him, but will remember those he does to others.

The great man won't do many things, because not very many things are worthy of him. But the things he does, he will do excellently, and they will be great things. He will never do anything secretly, nor hide his true feelings. This is what cowards do. So he always tells the truth. He has very few friends. Friends should be equals, and very few people are his equals. He doesn't praise or blame people. He would only praise people and their acts if they were better than his. On the other hand, he expects everyone else to behave worse, so why blame them?

Finally, a great man will walk slowly, speak evenly, and in a low tone, for to walk quickly and speak fast and in a high tone is a sign that you are excited and out of control. A great man thinks there is nothing worth getting excited and worried about.

Such, then, is the great man.

Notes *(while reading)*

Opening question *(after reading)*

Comments *(after discussion)*

40.   *Pensées,*
by B. Pascal

Although we know truths by our reason, we also know them through our heart. Through our heart we know the most basic truths. Reason, which has nothing to do with these first principles, tries to prove them wrong. It always fails. We know we are not dreaming when we are awake, although reason cannot prove it. This does not mean that we don't, after all, know we're awake. It just means that our reason is weak. Our knowledge of the most basic truths about space, time, motion, and numbers, is very certain. For its arguments, reason depends on such knowledge, which comes from our heart. The heart feels that space has three dimensions, and that there is an infinite series of numbers. Reason goes on from these truths to prove that if you square two numbers, no matter which ones they are, one square will not be twice the other. First principles are felt; propositions are proved. It is absurd for reason to demand from the heart proof of the most basic truths. It is just as absurd for the heart to demand from reason that all propositions feel true.

Reason would like to prove everything though it can't. It then tries to make us think that we are uncertain of the things it fails to prove. We should not let it. As if reason were the only way we learn! Sometimes we wish we didn't need reason at all, and knew everything simply by instinct and feeling. Unfortunately, human nature is not like that. We know very few things through instinct and feeling. Most of the things we know come through reason.

Notes *(while reading)*

Opening question *(after reading)*

Comments *(after discussion)*

41.   *Fragments,*

by Heraclitus

1. Your eyes and ears tell you lies if you don't understand inside.

2. To God all things are beautiful and good and just. But men have supposed some things to be just, other things unjust.

3. Someone said: "If only conflicts and struggle might be destroyed among gods and men." Heraclitus answered, "There would be no musical scale or music without high and low. There would be no life without male and female. But these are all opposites which struggle with each other."

4. All things move and shift. Nothing stays still. Everything is like a river and we cannot step into the same river twice.

5. My words are not as important as reason. Listen to it and you will agree that all things are one.

Notes (while reading)

Opening question (after reading)

Comments (after discussion)

42.   *Use and Abuse of History,*
by F. Nietzsche

Think about the herds of cattle that are feeding over there. They do not know the meaning of yesterday and today. From day to day, from morning to night, they roam and graze. Each day is taken up with the love and hate of the moment. They feel neither sadness nor satisfaction. Man, even though he is proud of being a man, cannot look on them without jealousy. Man wishes to live without sadness or satisfaction. But he will not change places with the cattle. He might ask one of the animals, "Why do you just look at me? Why don't you tell me about your happiness?" The cow might want to answer, "Because I always forget what I wanted to say." However, the animal forgets this answer also, and remains silent. The man can only wonder.

Man wonders also about himself. He cannot learn to forget. He hangs on to the past. The past moment returns like a ghost to haunt him, and it disturbs his rest. When this happens he says, "I remember". Then he is jealous once more of the animal which is able to forget. For the animal, each moment of time dies once it is past. The animal doesn't have a past. It doesn't have a history. It cannot lie, not can it hide anything. At every moment it is only what it is at that moment. Therefore, it is honest. However, man is always fighting against the weight of the past. The past presses down on him. When he talks with other men he tries to pretend his past is easier to live with than theirs. He lies to them about it to make them jealous. But when he sees a herd of cattle or a child playing he is hurt. It feels to him that he is looking on a paradise which he used to have, but which he has lost now. And yet, the child's play will soon end. It will end when it hears the words "once upon a time." With these words the child learns about battles and suffering. The child becomes a man. These words teach the child that human life cannot be lived completely in the present. Being human means being forced to remember the past. Memory makes it hard to be happy in the present moment. Death can stop the remembering. But death also destroys life and the present moment. This is what it means to be human.

Notes *(while reading)*

Opening question *(after reading)*

Comments *(after discussion)*

118

43. *"The Singing of Spirituals"*,
from *Horizon*

Lots was said in the press and elsewhere a few weeks back about the "revolt" of the students at Howard University in Washington DC. This "revolt" was against the singing of "Plantation Melodies".

The season for making up commencement and school-closing programs is now at hand. This prompts us to say a few words about one aspect of the matter which wasn't touched on much. We don't enter the case as a lawyer for either side but as a caretaker for the melodies.

First it should be said that few or none of the Plantation Melodies or Spirituals are "songs" or "Folk Songs". They are songs neither in the ordinary sense nor according to the dictionary definitions. Though crude, they are composed and sung as hymns in the religious worship or for private and personal consolation during times of sadness. Yet, it was claimed that the students were regularly called upon to perform these melodies for the "entertainment" of visitors. And, from their acts and associations, we can imagine how many of these famous and powerful people regard the soul-yearnings of our fathers and mothers. They look at them as the general public does the "living skeleton" and the "fat woman" in the circus sideshow. For them, Plantation Melodies and Spirituals are curious and "funny" things.

Again, however unique or expressive and beautiful may be the music or melody of some of these spirituals, one thing is clear. If they were changed to express correct and up-lifting thoughts or if they were written in proper language, their "popularity" with this class of visitors would quickly vanish. How much, for example, would these folks be

119

entertained or enraptured by the music, the really beautiful melody of "Steal Away," were it not for the wording, "I ain't got long to stay hyar". And where is the great popularity of "Roll, Jordan Roll," unless in its very confused theological geography—"I want to go to Heaven when I die, to hear sweet Jordan roll"?

These hymns, or some of them, express and show the cruel character of the oppression under which our fathers and mothers groaned. We can hear the hope and faith which kept our parents alive. We appreciate these melodies, we revere them. But we must not perform them season in and season out. To excite and tickle the entertainment needs of those who most want to hear them is to pervert their spirit and intent. It is close to sacrilege. Our visitors are touched by the spirituals as we would be by an Indian Ghost Dance or a Chinese funeral. If there were no other objection to their use for entertainment purposes, this would be an all-sufficient one.

Notes *(while reading)*

Opening question *(after reading)*

Comments (after discussion)

44.   *The Theory of Parallels,*
by N. Lobachevski

Through any point, for example A in the figure, many lines such as AE, AG, AH, AF, etc., can be drawn. With reference to yet another line, BC in the figure, the lines passing through point A can be divided into two groups. Some lines passing through point A cut that line BC. Other lines passing through A do not cut the line BC. The lines passing through point A therefore form two groups. We call these groups the *cutting* and *non-cutting groups* of lines. The boundary line of the group of non-cutting lines will be called the line *parallel to the given line, BC.*

From point A in the figure, we have dropped onto the line BC, the perpendicular line AD. To the line AD at the point A we have erected the perpendicular AE. In the right angle EAD, the straight lines which go out from point A either all will meet the line BC or some will not. An example of the group of cutting lines is the line AF. An example of the group of non-cutting lines is the perpendicular AE which does not meet the line BC.

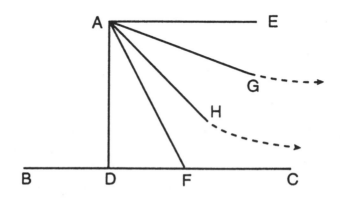

We will therefore assume it may be possible that there are still other lines passing through point A which do not cut the line BC. The line AG may be such a line which, however long it is made, does not cut BC.

In passing over from the cutting lines, such as AF, to the non-cutting lines, such as AG, we come upon a line AH which is a boundary line. On one side are all the lines like AF which meet the line BC. The line AH is the last line which does not cut BC, however long the lone AH and BC are made. It is the non-cutting line which we call the line through point A and parallel to the line BC.

Notes *(while reading)*

Opening question *(after reading)*

Comments (after discussion)

45. *"A Natural History of the German People"*, by George Eliot [Mary Ann Evans]

Art is the nearest thing to life. It is a way of increasing our experience and extending our contact with our fellow men beyond the bounds of our personal lives. So the artist's or novelist's task is sacred when he treats the life of People. Falsification here is far more evil than in the more artificial parts of life. It is not so very serious that we should have false ideas about the short-lived fashions of a duchess. But it is serious that our sympathy with the ever-recurring joys and struggles, the toil, the tragedy, and the humor in the life of our more oppressed fellow men should be perverted. Our feeling must not be directed by the artist towards a false object instead of the true one.

The perversion of our sympathy is not the less deadly because the false picture which gives rise to it has what the novelist considers a moral purpose. The thing for mankind—all of us—to know is not what are the motives and influences which the novelist thinks *ought* to act on the laborer or workman. Instead, we must know what are the motives and influences which *do* act on him. We don't want to be taught to feel for an imagined heroic workman or romanticized farmer. Rather, we must learn to feel for the actual farmer in all his coarse indifference and the real workman in all his suspicious selfishness.

We need the novelist's true idea of the common people's character to guide our feelings rightly. We also need it to check our social theories and direct us in their application. Our theories are of three types. The first theory comes from the tendency created by the great and splendid conquests of modern science. This holds that all social

125

questions are really part of the science of economics. This theory claims that the relations of men with their neighbors may be settled by algebraic and scientific equations. The second type of theory is really a dream. Some people pretend that the poorer classes are now ready for a higher condition which can be based principally in their present moral feelings. The third type of theory is the aristocratic attempt to restore the "good old days". None of these three different mistakes can co-exist with a real knowledge of the People, with a thorough study of their habits, their ideas, and their motives.

This thorough study can only be presented to us as a novel. But in addition it requires a very special novelist. The writer must be someone of very wide moral and intellectual scope. He must devote himself to studying the natural history of our social classes. He should observe how local conditions influence them, the rules of their actions and their habits, how they view their religious teachers and how they are influenced by their religious beliefs. But, most importantly, his work will only be of assistance to us if he has neither foregone conclusions nor the point of view of any particular profession.

Notes *(while reading)*

Opening question *(after reading)*

Comments *(after discussion)*

All the perceptions of the human mind are of two kinds. I call these kinds *Impressions* and *Ideas*. They differ from each other in the amount of force and liveliness with which they strike the mind. Those perceptions which are most forceful and violent, we may call *impressions*. These are our sensations—the colors we see, the hardness we touch, etc.—and our emotions as they first appear in the soul. By *ideas*, I mean the faint images of these impressions in our thought. For instance, the perceptions excited by reading these words are ideas. The perceptions excited by touching the page and by seeing the black and white of the print are impressions. I don't believe many words are needed to explain this difference. Everyone readily realizes the difference between feeling or sensation and thinking.

The difference between ideas and impressions is generally very noticeable. Yet, it is not impossible in certain cases that they closely approach one another. In sleep, in a fever, in cases of madness or in instances of violent emotions in our soul, our ideas may approach the forcefulness of an impression. On the other hand, our impressions can be so faint and weak that it is hard to distinguish them from ideas. Nevertheless, in spite of cases of this kind, they are in general very different. No one could avoid admitting these perceptions are of two different kinds. It is therefore right to give each a name to indicate the difference.

There is another difference among our perceptions which concerns both impressions and ideas. The division is into Simple and Complex. Simple perceptions, either impressions or ideas, are ones which can not be separated into parts. The complex ideas or impressions can be separated into parts. Though a color, a taste, and a smell are all united in an apple, it is easy to see that these qualities can be separated. The apple, as an impression we see and touch or as an idea we think of, is complex. The color, taste, and smell are simple perceptions.

We can now consider the relations between impressions and ideas. What first strikes my eye is the great similarity between our ideas and our impressions in every respect except forcefulness and liveliness. The one kind seems to be a reflection of the other. All the perceptions of the mind are double. They appear as ideas and impressions. When I close my eyes and think about my room, the ideas I form are exact copies of the impressions I felt. There is nothing in one which is not found in the other. Ideas and impressions appear always to correspond to each other.

However, the more I think about this the more I find I was carried away by the first appearances. I must make use of the distinction of perceptions into simple and complex to limit my claim that all our ideas and impressions resemble each other. Many of our complex ideas never had impressions that correspond to them. Many of our complex impressions are never copied in ideas. I can imagine a city like New Jerusalem whose streets are gold and whose walls are rubies, though I have never seen such a place. On the other hand, I have seen Paris, but do not have an idea which represents the impressions I have had of that city. When we consider our simple perceptions, we find, just as I said, that every simple idea does have a simple impression which resembles it. Every simple impression has a corresponding idea.

Notes *(while reading)*

Opening question *(after reading)*

Comments *(after discussion)*

47. *The Manual,*
by Epictetus

Some things are in our power and control, while others aren't. It is in our power to decide what we think about things, and to decide which things we are going to pursue. It is also in our power to decide what we like and don't like. In a word, we control our own actions. Outside our power and control are all bodies in the world including even our own bodies, and our own property. Also, we have no control over our reputations, and no control over whether people listen to us or not. Again, in a word, what are not our own actions.

The things which are in our power are by nature free. Those which are not in our power are weak, slavish, and belong to others. Remember then, if you start thinking that slavish things are free, or that what belongs to others belongs to you, you will feel trapped. You will blame both gods and men. But if you suppose that what really belongs to you *does* belong to you, and that what really belongs to another *does* belong to another, you will be free. No one will ever force you. No one can ever stop you. You won't ever blame anyone for anything. You'll do nothing against your own will. You will have no enemies, because no one will be able to hurt you.

If you decide to pursue such great things, you must also decide not to be attracted by money, property, reputation, and all the other things which are outside your control. You must give up some of them completely. The others you must postpone for the time being.

If you want to be free, to have no enemies, to do nothing against your will, and at the same time to rule and control others and be rich, you will surely fail. You can become free and happy only if you gain power and control over yourself.

Notes *(while reading)*

Opening question *(after reading)*

Comments (after discussion)

133

48. *About the Soul,*
by Aristotle

Things which are alive have souls. Things which do not have souls are not alive. We say that something is alive if any one of the following powers is present in it: intelligence, motion from place to place, sensing, that is, seeing, hearing, touching, etc., and finally the power to take in food and grow, that is, nutrition. Plants are clearly alive because they can absorb food from the ground. This allows them to grow and reproduce themselves. A living thing may have the ability to nourish itself without having any of the other powers of the soul. Plants are like this. However, no living thing has these other powers without also having the ability to nourish itself.

These powers of the soul thus form a series from lower to higher. The higher powers depend on the lower. For example, a living thing can't have the power of sensing without also having the ability to nourish itself. Again, a living thing cannot have the power of moving from place to place, unless it also has the power of sensing where it is going. Finally, there are some living things which have the ability to think. These must have all the other powers of soul.

The ability to nourish itself belongs to all living things. We must, therefore, discuss it first. Because it possesses this power, the living thing can nourish itself and thus grow and reproduce. The most natural activity of a living thing is to produce another one like itself. An animal gives birth to an animal like itself. Living things do this so they can have a share in the eternal and divine, as far as they are able.

Everything strives to be like the eternal and divine, and everything which it does naturally, it does for the sake of this. Living things cannot share in the eternal and divine by themselves living forever. So, they do the best they can by leaving behind others who are like themselves.

Notes *(while reading)*

Opening question *(after reading)*

Comments *(after discussion)*

136

49.   *The Second Treatise of Government,*
by J. Locke

How could anyone ever come to own anything, that is, have property? This question appears a great difficulty to some writers. I, however, will try to show that property can emerge out of what God gave everyone in common. In fact, I will show that this even occurred without any written or spoken agreement among people.

God gave the world to all people in common. He has also given us reason and thought to make use of the things in the world to stay alive and even improve our lives. The earth and everything on it were first given to us for our support and comfort. All the fruits it naturally produces and the animals it feeds belonged to everyone in common. No one had a private rule or right over anything in the original natural state of human beings. Yet, fruits and animals are on the earth for our use. There must therefore be a way that a particular person can rightly acquire some fruit or animals in order actually to use them for his benefit. The fruit or meat which a wild Indian eats must first become his possession so that others no longer have a right to it. Otherwise, how can it do him any good for keeping himself alive. If there is no way for him rightfully to eat fruit, then eating fruit would always mean stealing it from everyone else.

By nature, the earth and all the lower animals are the common possession of everyone. However, each person owns himself. No one has a right to his person but himself. The labor of his body and the work of his hands are therefore also properly his. Whatever he himself removes from nature has thereby been mixed with which was already his own and made what he removed his property. By his labor he has joined to the fruit something which excludes everyone else. A person's labor is without any question his own property. No one but he can have a right to what it is joined to. This is true at least where there is still enough fruit left for others to use.

A person who picks apples from a tree in the woods which no one owns and eats them has certainly made them his own. The nourishment is his. I ask when did the apples begin to be his? When he ate them or digested them or when he brought them home? It's plain that if the first gathering of the apples didn't make them his, nothing else could. His labor made those apples different from all others. He added to those apples something more than nature had done. They then became his private property.

Notes *(while reading)*

Opening question *(after reading)*

Comments (after discussion)

50. *The Republic*, Bk. VII,
by Plato

Socrates is speaking with his young friend, Glaucon.

Socrates: Glaucon, let's try to think about what human life is like ordinarily, and what it might be like for someone who somehow got to know the truth about it. Imagine that all human beings live in a cave under the earth. The cave has an entrance open to the light of day. But the human beings are chained so that they can neither move, nor turn toward the opening, nor even turn toward each other. They have been chained in this way since their childhood. Imagine also that there is a fire burning and glowing within the cave. It is above and behind the prisoners, casting shadows on the wall in front of them. They cannot see the fire. All the prisoners can see are shadows of themselves and of each other on the wall. They also see shadows cast by anything that is carried behind their backs between the glowing fire and themselves.

Glaucon: This is a strange image, Socrates, and the prisoners are strange prisoners.

Soc: In many ways, these prisoners are just like us. Do you think these people will see anything of themselves or each other except the shadows cast on the wall?

Glau: No, not if they are not able to look in any direction except straight ahead.

Soc: And what about the things carried past them, behind their backs? Would they see those things themselves, or only their shadows? Even worse, could they even know if they were missing something?

Glau: No, perhaps they could not tell the difference.

Soc: Would their conversations with each other be about anything real? Wouldn't they think that the shadows were real things?

Glau: Yes, of course.

Soc: Could these people ever be freed and healed of their ignorance?

Glau: I don't know.

Soc: What if something like this happened? I'm not sure how it would happen. Suppose one prisoner was freed from his chains, and forced suddenly to stand up, to turn around, to look, and try to walk. Wouldn't he be confused and frightened when he saw the glow of the fire, and when he saw the objects which cast the shadows he had been looking at before? But, what if he were forced to go on? Suppose he were dragged out into the light of day. Wouldn't he be frightened and confused again, as he saw the things that exist in the light of day, in the light of the sun? All he had seen before were shadows of things by firelight. Now he has to look upon things in the sun. At first, he couldn't look directly at these things, but, he could look at their shadows and at their reflections in ponds. After a while, he could look directly at the things in the light of the sun. Finally, after much difficulty, he would be able to look with gladness upon the sun itself.

How might the person who had gone through this journey think about where he had been before, and where he

141

was now? I guess that the first part of his life might not seem so important anymore. His recent discoveries might seem like the most important things in the world. Also, after he thought about it, he might suspect that his fellow prisoners would not be glad to see him again, especially if they thought he knew something they didn't. They would especially resent him if he told them that the things they have spent their lives getting good at are unreal and unimportant. They might laugh at him because he was no longer good at dealing with things in the cave. Finally, they might even act from their resentment and try to kill him. Still, down again he must go, since he knows he has something good to offer his fellow-prisoners, and he must try to learn how to do that as well as he can.

Glau: If human life really is like life in the cave, then I can see why it would be dangerous for someone who had learned the truth about things to try to return to help those still there.

Notes (while reading)

Opening question (after reading)

Comments (after discussion)